CREATE YOUR
EXTRAORDINARY LIFE
NOW!

CREATE YOUR EXTRAORDINARY LIFE
NOW!

ANDREA COLANDREA & BOB LEMBO

iUniverse, Inc.
Bloomington

Create Your Extraordinary Life NOW!

iUniverse books may be ordered through booksellers or by contacting:

iUniverse
1663 Liberty Drive
Bloomington, IN 47403
www.iuniverse.com
1-800-Authors (1-800-288-4677)

ISBN: 978-1-4759-7266-5 (sc)
ISBN: 978-1-4759-7267-2 (ebk)

Printed in the United States of America

iUniverse rev. date: 03/18/2013

CONTENTS

This book is dedicated to my Nonno Luigi my mom and dad and all the moms and dads in the world and the one that makes it all happen God.

"The most beautiful people we have known are those who have known defeat, known suffering, known struggle, known loss, and have found their way out of the depths. These persons have an appreciation, a sensitivity, and an understanding of life that fills them with compassion, gentleness, and a deep loving concern. Beautiful people do not just happen."
— Elisabeth Kübler-Ross

"Life is an opportunity, benefit from it.
Life is beauty, admire it.
Life is a dream, realize it.
Life is a challenge, meet it.
Life is a duty, complete it.
Life is a game, play it.
Life is a promise, fulfill it.
Life is sorrow, overcome it.
Life is a song, sing it.
Life is a struggle, accept it.
Life is a tragedy, confront it.
Life is an adventure, dare it.
Life is luck, make it.
Life is too precious, do not destroy it.
Life is life, fight for it."
— Mother Teresa

INTRODUCTION

It was February 2001 when I got my divorce papers from court. I thought my life had come to an end. What went wrong? I pondered over what I could have done to cause this over and over again. I was married to a beautiful girl who loved me, I was extremely successful in business, I was close to my family, and everything seemed right, but I knew deep inside that something was wrong. I just did not know what.

I could not understand the empty feeling inside me. I was very successful, so I did what most successful people do: I enjoyed the fruits of my labor by spending money on vacations, cars, boats, romantic gateways, and whatever I thought would make me happy. At times when I would dare to surrender my ego and have the courage to admit that there was something wrong, I would ask the people I loved what was wrong with me. For example, my mom would say, "Nothing is wrong with you. You're the best son a mom could have, and I am so proud of you. I think it's the stress from your business partners."

At the time I was partners in a chain of pizzerias and was at times very stressful so I thought my mom could be right. Next, I asked my wife what she taught was wrong with me. She said, "Honey, nothing is wrong with you. I am so happy to be with you and I love you." She also assumed that I was happy also. But for some reason I wasn't. My sisters were the best. They would say, "Andre, as you get older, you are not as happy as when you were a kid its just life. What you are experiencing is normal." So I thought about what a bummer it was to get older and be an adult. I was not liking my life at all even worse I hated my life and wanted to die.

Then I began thinking, *Thank God I have money and a wife who validates me.* This kind of thinking caused me to cover up my true feelings of sadness, anger, rage, and shame and made me need more more money, and more of everything else I could get my hands on. As a result, I developed a few addictions.

As I continued to indulge in my overeating, and overspending and other things I could indulge in, I however realized that my sadness was not and did not go away. As a result of my addictions and bad behavior, my marriage slowly but surely came to an end. I got divorced in 2001.

After I got divorced, my whole world came crashing down. I no longer had money. I had to sell my business to pay for my divorce, and my inability to focus made making money harder.

My wife, who used to validate me, was not there anymore. I got so depressed that I did not have enough confidence to even pursue a new girl. After all, who wants to be with someone who is sad and depressed? I was still addicted to food, but I soon realized that being fat did not help with having no money, no confidence and meeting someone seemed impossible and that made things even worse.

The journey to build my life back began on Valentine's Day 2001, when I attended a workshop about death and dying with Susan Anderson. This journey from misery to creating an extraordinary life was full of ups and downs, but I would not change it for the world.

For the first time, I was not living a double life. Also, I started to honor what was going on inside me and began to understand myself and what made me tick. The experience taught me a few things. The first is that I know very little. The second is that the little that I do know is always changing. The third is that when I think I know it all, I need to step back, reevaluate my life, and realize that I might be off track again.

Throughout this journey, I met many great people who have had a great influence on me. One of the great people I've met is Bob. When I met Bob, he was a customer in the pizzeria I owned, and we soon became friends. Bob, just like the rest of us, has struggled with his own journey to rebuild his life and build a life he loves.

Over the years, Bob and I took many drives to the beach and had many lunches at diners. As time went on, we both grew to love each other as the best of friends. We would always share what we had learned that made our lives worth living.

In 2008, I had a show on a local cable network called *Creating an Extraordinary Life*. I would interview people about how they created extraordinary lives for themselves. That's where I got the idea to write a book about it. Soon after I started to write the book, I realized that many of the philosophies I had were due to my conversations with Bob, so I decided to ask him if he would be a coauthor of the book, and he agreed. The title of the book became *Create Your Extraordinary Life Now*. This book is about those conversations Bob and I had over the years. One thing Bob and I agreed on was the commitment to reach out to all people regardless of their sex, age, status, or nationality or any other difference a person may have. We are all children of God and all worthy and deserving of creating an extraordinary life. Also, we agreed that nothing we say is set in stone. As we change our inner reality, our outer reality and understanding of life will also change. So when you read this book, we urge you to take what you like and leave the rest.

We hope and believe that this book can help you create the life you love and deserve and the life that God wants you to live. We urge you to not just read the book but also practice the concepts, note what touches you inside, and highlight what you think you can use. We provided spaces for you to take notes at the end of the book. If you need more space, buy a notebook and take notes each day. Try the some or all the ideas concepts we suggest for thirty days. We believe you will be much happier and on your way to a life created by you and a life you love. Another thing we agreed on is that it takes courage to live the life you love.

You may not agree with some things you read in this book today until years from now. This has been my experience with many things I have read over time. Sometimes what works for you today may not work for you tomorrow. I believe you will get whatever you need at the time you are ready to get it.

We have developed our philosophy over many years by reading many books, attending workshops, having thousands of conversations, coaching others, and getting coaching ourselves.

We urge you to make a commitment to yourself before you start to read this book to create an extraordinary life and not to stop reading until you are living the life you love that is what we done and still do each day.

My friends, Bob and I want to wish you good luck on your journey. Remember, having an extraordinary life is your birthright.

"You don't love someone because they're perfect, you love them in spite of the fact that they're not."
— Jodi Picoult, *My Sister's Keeper*

"I wanted a perfect ending. Now I've learned, the hard way, that some poems don't rhyme, and some stories don't have a clear beginning, middle, and end. Life is about not knowing, having to change, taking the moment and making the best of it, without knowing what's going to happen next. Delicious Ambiguity."
— Gilda Radner

YOU ARE PERFECT
JUST THE WAY YOU ARE

On our journey toward realizing happiness, we must always know clearly and completely that we are perfect at all times. Regardless of what has happened in the past, we are perfect just the way we are and just the way we are not. Any time we are working on ourselves, it's not because we are not perfect but because we want to grow in a particular area of our life that inspires us.

If we think of ourselves as being perfect at all times, we can then take responsibility for our lives without making us wrong. When we do something that is not in line with the person we want to be, we can just accept it, make amends to ourselves or others, and move on. Apologizing should be easy because making that apology does not mean that there is something wrong with us. It just means that we acknowledge that something we did is not in line with the person we want to be and the life we want to live. Unfulfilled people tend to be unable to admit that they are complete and perfect. This is because of the fear of accepting ourselves as who we are now and not as our ideal vision of who we want to be. This could not be further from the truth. Declaring completeness and wholeness as a perfect individual can help us achieve our life goals much more easily because it means we can make decisions based on what we are committed to in life and not based on our egos. Our egos are always going to tell us that there is something wrong. This is how the ego survives, as Eckhart Tolle writes in *The Power of Now*.

To change our programming from believing that we are not perfect to believing that we are perfect at all times will take some time. As children, we were taught that there is something wrong with us or what we have done. It is possible to change that negative programming. A great place to start is by using affirmations daily, reminding ourselves that we are perfect, whole, and complete. God loves us just the way we are, and we are God's children.

Remember that changing some aspect of ourselves, like losing weight, making more money, or getting a nose job, does not mean we are changing "the being of ourselves." Our "being," our soul, is perfect at all times regardless of what we do or do not do, what we have accomplished, how much money we have, or our degrees, looks, or statuses.

To accept ourselves entails pure love and happiness. Once we can accept ourselves 100 percent as perfect, whole, and complete, we can also accept others. We cannot love one another until we love ourselves. If we are waiting to be perfect, it will never happen because we are already perfect.

Many people take their own lives' incomplete circumstances and situations as an indication of their own incompleteness. For example, we confuse the desire to lose ten pounds with the need to lose ten pounds in order to be perfect. Another example is that the idea that once I find the perfect woman or man, I will be happy. This is a defective, wrong, negative, destructive, and disempowering way of thinking. Only by affirming that we are whole, perfect, and complete just as we are can we freely improve ourselves without the stress of feeling incomplete.

The person who chooses never to change is as perfect and whole as the one who chooses to change. I know that this is hard for some of us to accept, but it's the truth. Everyone, regardless of what they do or do not do, is always perfect, whole, and complete. People who have a problem with this statement usually have a problem accepting the people around them and have lots of stress in their lives, especially in their relationships. Are you one of them? Once you can see others and yourself as perfect at all times, most of your problems in relationships will disappear. You will be a happier person with a happier life.

"Never doubt that a small group of thoughtful, committed, citizens can change the world. Indeed, it is the only thing that ever has."
— Margaret Mead

COMMITMENT IS THE KEY TO A LIFE WORTH LIVING

Commitment is a strong pledge or uncompromising pact with oneself. It is a vow to be seriously engaged with an idea that we are resolved to achieve.

This concept of commitment is fundamental to achieving an extraordinary life because it is the very engine that will drive you toward that achievement. It is a call to action and the compelling force required to bring focus in your life.

Action is all that matters. The rest is philosophy. Philosophy makes us think and sets the stage, but it causes no change. Change only comes through action, and focused commitment is the vehicle that will take you there.

Commitment also summons a quality from within whose virtue is to create the space in which keeping your word can happen. A commitment to keeping your word is necessary.

Commitment is not an act of will but rather a condition that we bring into existence. It is a declaration that defines us, which allows all other goals and ideas to be fulfilled.

Commitment is not to be confused with intention. Intention is an idea that may cause doubt in our ability to follow through, whereas commitment is an unshakeable trust derived from deep within our soul that will allow our intention to be fulfilled. It is the quality that we must acquire to bridge the gap between wanting and having, between a mediocre life and a life worth living.

We are not born with commitment. We find it as we evolve as people. We then realize that our dreams can only become reality if we first pledge to keep our word to ourselves to achieve what we are committed to in life. When we are willing to create and to be committed to making our dreams a reality, we will be impelled by that commitment achieve our goals.

Think of yourself as an arrow speeding toward a target with a purpose and control you never thought possible. Commitment is the bow that releases you toward your goal. It is the all-important element that sets up the space between the bow and the target to be crossed in a straight line so that it hits the bull's-eye.

The stronger the conviction of commitment we have, the easier it will be to hit our mark.

To have proper focus, we must ask exactly what our commitment will provide. There is no room for judgment of what we want to achieve, just an intense focus on precisely what we want to have happen. Visualize your goal as if it has already happened and is part of your reality. The subconscious mind cannot distinguish between what is happening and what we want to happen.

It is also important to make a distinction between our wants and needs. Wants come and go, needs are required to sustain our life and survive, but commitments define our lives and make them worth living.

Finally, we must position our commitment in the present moment and keep it real each day. Once we give birth to our commitments, we must renew them, feed them, water them, and keep them alive.

"Success is not final, failure is not fatal: it is the courage to continue that counts."
— Winston Churchill

THE COURAGE TO BE RESPONSIBLE FOR YOUR LIFE AND CREATE THE LIFE YOU LOVE

Responsibility should be seen as the unwavering, proactive response to the acknowledgement of your actions as the sole cause and reason for everything in your life. This means that you are the only person responsible for all that happens in your life.

To be responsible, one must have courage. It takes courage to be responsible and to admit that you had a part in everything that happens in your life. Being responsible to yourself is the only way you can make changes in your life that will guarantee success. You must act positively to ensure you have a life worth living. Responsibility will give you the fearlessness to propel your commitment and goals to success. This claimed and reclaimed commitment will give you the focus and drive necessary to fulfill your dreams.

Most people have a negative way of looking at responsibility. If you feel bad about something or beat yourself up about something, you are not being responsible. You are playing a victim role that serves no one in a positive matter. One way to be responsible for your life is to accept everything that happens to you and accept that in some way that you had a part in it.

The truth is, you are the cause of everything you do and everything that's done to you. Yes, things that are done to you are drawn to you as the consequences of what you cause to happen, just as metal shavings are drawn to a magnet. This is hard for most to accept, and that is why many people stay in the victim role for years or their entire lives. To accept full responsibility is to take back full control. It does not matter whether you are right or wrong. What matters is that you get your life under control so you can create a life worth living, and that is done by being responsible and not being a victim. That is why it is so important to constantly be aware of your commitment to accept total responsibility in all your actions. Once you accept full responsibility, you will no longer be a victim, and you will have full power.

Responsibility lives in the present moment. It is the action, not the reaction. Talking about what happened in the past or what someone has done to you does nothing for your future. Sometimes to be responsible you may have to hurt someone emotionally or do something other people may not like. There is no way of being halfway responsible for your life. Either you are responsible and accountable or not.

The things that you take responsibility for will create a willful path toward accessing your life goals. This is because you will be the cause. The things you don't take responsibility for can go in any direction since you will be at the mercy of the effect of your own indecision, whose outcomes will be brought to you and not by you. To relinquish ownership of your actions is to live an uncontrollable life. Although you cannot control other people, places, or things, you can control yourself or at the very least be responsible for yourself.

There are no excuses. This includes being responsible for your failures so you can make necessary adjustments and move forward toward your life goals. Failures should be seen as points of alteration to redirect your efforts in a more useful way. Being responsible for your failures is a necessary for creating your extraordinary life.

Failure should be welcomed, but accepting failure does not make you wrong. Ultimately, you are responsible for the gap between what you want and what it takes to get there. You must be the source of everything that happens in your life and be accountable for it.

Responsibility is the foundation of commitment. Commitment without responsibility is like a house on a weak foundation. It will be subject to all the pressures of nature and eventually fall down under the weight of its instability. Having a strong foundation of responsibility will allow your house to endure whatever comes your way because you will be standing on firm ground that may bend but will never break on your inevitable road to success.

"You are never too old to set another goal or to dream a new dream."
— C.S. Lewis

Commitments vs. Goals

As mentioned in the previous chapter, commitment is the key to a powerful life worth living. Commitment is not to be confused with goals. Goals are what we create and set for ourselves to accomplish our life commitments. Commitments are what define us in life. Commitments are what we stand for in life and what make our lives worth living. Our commitments must also be free from any attachments.

You may have a commitment to having a loving family but be attached to assigning conditions that only satisfy your ego, fears, and insecurities. For example, you want to have a girlfriend or boyfriend whom you connect with on every level, but you have an attachment to the way your partner looks, how much money he or she has, or what his or her education level is, just because you want the approval of your family and friends. That attachment will surely keep you from attaining your goal. Your low self-worth is creating an unhealthy attachment and forming a barrier to your goal of meeting a person that would make a good match for you. Deal with your insecurities first and then your goal will materialize.

Once your goals are free from any attachments, fears, or insecurities, you will accomplish them. This will also allow your creative energy to flow naturally, which will make your life easier and happier.

People who are attached rarely get anything done because they are more concerned about their attachments (insecurities, fears, worries about looking good, desires to avoiding obstacles, etc.) than about accomplishing the goal they have created so they can feel alive.

Worrying about what others think also taps into your creative power and is counterproductive.

You must always create your commitments before setting your goals. The order should be life commitments, long-term goals, short-term goals, and, finally, the daily to-do list. All must be flowing in the same direction. For example, to have a life commitment of being healthy while also having a goal of eating whatever you want, anytime you want may be counterproductive.

To summarize, check all your commitments to see if your goals are in line with your commitments. Once your goals are in line with your commitments, achieving your goals will flow freely.

NOTES

"It is good to have an end to journey toward; but it is the journey that matters, in the end."

— Ernest Hemingway

ACCOMPLISHING
YOUR LIFE'S PURPOSE

We are all born the same: pure and full of love and dreams. All we want to do is enjoy life and be happy. But along the road of life we encounter experiences that we have no explanations for. What happened? What went wrong? It all started with a simple experience. For example, as a baby it could be as simple as being hungry, crying, and not being fed immediately. As a youngster, it could be being made fun of. Later on in life, it could be being criticized

We end up blaming ourselves for things we can't understand that happen to us. We become victims to our diminishing self-image and self-worth. We get further and further away from that pure being that was born full of love for life with no baggage of guilt, remorse, self-pity, or other negative emotions.

We keep blaming ourselves, life, and God. As a result, we build a picture of who we think we are and what life is all about until the happiness that is our birthright is a distant memory.

We must stop living our lives through the actions of our past and start creating a reality out of the possibilities of the present moment. We must be the causes of our lives, not the effects. Acknowledging ourselves as a perfect creation of God just the way we are right now (the parts we like about ourselves and the part we don't like about ourselves) will give us the ability to forgive ourselves and others for the past and present and create the life we love and deserve.

Where do we start? We can start by making a list of the things that inspire us in life. Inspiration, also known as purpose, is very different than wants and needs. A want is a desire, such as for a new car. A need is a requirement, such as food, water, and shelter. Inspiration or life purpose is something that drives you and defines you. Good questions to ask is to find your inspiration are, While on your deathbed, what do you want to be recognized for? What do you want to be remembered for? What contribution do you want to make in the world?

When planning out your life, start with the end first and work backward. For example, begin with your life purpose. Then continue with long-term goals that are coherent and in line with your life purpose. Once a year, write down your yearly goals and make sure they are in line with your life purpose. Each month, write down your monthly goals and make sure they are in line with your yearly goals. Each week, write down your weekly goals and make sure they are in line with your monthly goals.

Here a few suggestions to help you be accountable for setting goals and keeping them. First, join a goal-setting group or create a goal-setting group yourself. Second, hire a life coach to guide through your goal-setting process and to be accountable. Third, having good role models and mentors in your life will help inspire you to follow through with your goals. If you don't have a role model or mentor, you can use someone who inspires you, such as an author, motivational speaker, or entrepreneur.

We must see our goals as if we had already realized them. Make no mistake about it: On the road to realizing our dreams, there will be challenges and obstacles. When the going gets tough, we must recommit ourselves to our goals. We must accept the responsibility of our lives with renewed enthusiasm and conviction.

Make challenges a positive experience by saying to yourself, *I am learning something different each time I go through a challenge. Every challenge is a necessity for my growth.* A life worth living may seem easy at times and not so easy at other times, but once we have our commitments and purpose clear, we will do whatever it takes to create the life we love.

"The happiness of your life depends upon the quality of your thoughts."
— Marcus Aurelius, *Meditations*

THE SUBCONSCIOUS MIND AND MAKING REAL CHANGE IN YOUR LIFE

Before techniques can be utilized for self-improvement, it is essential to understand how the mind works and where your power lies to make lasting change possible. The conscious mind is analytical and highly critical of all the information it receives. This reasoning component makes judgments and stores these judgments in the subconscious mind as beliefs whether they are true or not.

Your subconscious mind is a goal-striving, completely impersonal mechanism whose sole intent is to create the reality that you set for yourself, filtered through your self-image. It works automatically, with no judgment, toward goals of success or failure. It dutifully allows for an outcome to perfectly coincide with who you think you are. If you feed information into the subconscious saying that you are unworthy, inferior, guilt ridden, etc., it will accept this information as truth and ensure that your reality reflects that image as an objective experience. If you feed information saying that you are worthy, expect success, have self-love, etc., it will likewise accept that as truth and propel you to actions that ensure success. You can do nothing other than reflect into the world the results of your self-image.

In effect, all our actions are predetermined by desires that must be filtered through our self-image before they can be realized. Conscious desires cannot be fulfilled unless they reflect an alignment to that image. In fact, there is no choice after desires are filtered, because the result has to be, at all times, a perfect reflection of your self-image. The wonderful lesson here is that as you acquire a better picture of yourself, this picture becomes the filter that creates your reality.

Think about it. No matter how hard you might try to accomplish even the most ordinary things, unless your goals are consistent with your self-image, they will be processed and rejected, and your actions will ensure failure. Goals that are consistent will produce actions that succeed.

Our subconscious mind has been faithfully recording all of our thoughts and experiences since birth, recording into our memory everything we experienced and felt in a completely impersonal manner, based on our perception of what happened. It doesn't matter if we remember these experiences or not. It doesn't matter if we feel we are different now. Everything gets recorded. And everything has an impact on our present moment's reality because it all gets filtered through our self-image.

In his groundbreaking book *Psycho-cybernetics*, Dr. Maxwell Maltz gives an example of how our subconscious, from our earliest years, affects us now. There are three components to memory that have varying impacts on our self-image: authoritative source, intensity, and repetition. An authoritative source for a child might be a father whom we see as a God figure and desperately seek acceptance from. If your father screamed at you that you were useless and no good, you would accept that as truth because of your complete belief in his infallibility. You would probably blame yourself because you had no other answer. If he screamed at you in front of family and friends, that would intensify the impact of that memory on your subconscious and what it did to your self-image. You would feel even worse about yourself and might start to build up a defense mechanism to deal with it. If he repeatedly screamed at you on a daily basis, that repetition would have a huge impact on your self-image that, if not dealt with, would undoubtedly be a factor in your reality.

The importance of a good self-image cannot be overstated. It is the primary, fundamental factor on which other techniques of motivation are based. Everything gets filtered through that image, and the results must correspond regardless of their intent. The creative power we all have resides in the love of self we have had from birth. We must strive to overcome a self-image that has been battered by our interpretations of our life's experiences and the unbalanced, disorganized people we have become as a result. Acquiring a strong self-image allows us to regain the strong creative power that is our birthright. Once our positive creative power is restored, our desires will be easily met.

So how do we start to build a good self-image? To begin with, this chapter is designed to give you a brief knowledge of how the mind works so you have a good starting point to embark from. Knowing how your mind works should answer many misconceptions about how we process and store information, and this understanding should show that the only way to change our external reality is to change our inner reality.

Self-confidence must be restored and self-doubt cast away as the illusion it really is. Self-acceptance does not mean changing yourself but rather changing your mental picture and realizing that self from the inside. With acceptance and self-confidence, your insecurities will fall away because they will be inconsistent with your new image. Resentments will be a thing of the past because jealousy and victimization will not be necessary as excuses for our perceived failures. Ultimately you will utilize the greatest of all personal tools, forgiveness. To be able to forgive yourself and others is the most emotional ally freeing gift you can give yourself.

What do you need to forgive yourself for? We are all humans and are doing the best we can on this journey called our life. What will remorse and regret do for you or others? Is feeling guilty helping you or others? If you truly want to make a difference in this world, you must find the courage to forgive yourself and others. Forgiveness is truly the highest level of wisdom. We must take complete responsibility as being the cause for all the actions of our life without assigning blame or guilt and move on. Admit your mistakes, learn from them, and release them.

Emotions are needed to help us respond to reality in the present moment. The past cannot be relived, and dwelling on past events can only impede your present progress. In fact, as you acquire a stronger self-image, those same events that you now remember as hurtful and emotionally scarring will come to be seen in a completely different light, reflecting an understanding based on your new perception of reality. Remember, your conception of the past is not set in stone. Things that happened in the past were filtered through your past self-image. You will understand the past differently as you forgive yourself and others and learn to change your inner reality.

Everyone is on a personal journey and is conflicted in his or her own way. Negative things that are done to us by others will always be engaged by our self-image. A bad self-image will always produce a defensive emotional reaction based on insecurities within ourselves. That is the way humans are made. A good self-image will breed compassion and understanding. We will no longer need to feel sorry for ourselves or enjoy condemning others. In fact, true forgiveness will come with the realization that there was nothing to forgive in the first place.

Everything that has ever happened to you was a blessing in disguise, for your past experiences have formed a platform for the present moment. With this new wisdom, you can now begin to practice loving yourself unconditionally. You have caused yourself to be reading this chapter now for a reason. Take the opportunity of what this present moment is offering you and use it as a first step toward a happy, successful life.

NOTES

"Our life is what our thoughts make it."
— Marcus Aurelius, *Meditations*

Positive Self-Image Equals a Happy Reality

Most people think they make choices, but most of the time our choices are made for us. The human mind requires us to have both sides of every issue in front of us in order to consciously make a choice. In order for us to think of something, our brain, through its memory, weighs everything we have learned about from the issue since birth and then decides what it means. This happens in a fraction of a second in all our conscious thoughts, whether trivial or important. Worst of all, we are not aware of this process.

What we think are choices are really actions based on decisions already made. These decisions usually are made based on the past, so this opens up the question, Are we really ever choosing?

The truth, or what we call the truth, must be filtered through the image we have of ourselves before it becomes our conscious reality.

What we call reality and truth is only, can only, and will always only be a reflection of our self-image. Simply put, the better our self-image, the better our reality, and the happier our life will be.

Our actions are decided by our self-image, which has been formed by our subconscious, and then consciously acted out in our reality, which is in the present moment. We are always living in a universe of the past moment whose actions are predetermined by the filter of self-image.

Our vision of any situation is always manipulated to mirror the image we have of ourselves. If we want to change our reality, we must first change our self-image. A changed self-image will change our decisions and choices and then the direction of our life.

A bad self-image will always produce decisions that are not good for us while a positive self-image will always produce decisions that are good for us. It has to always be this way, because perception of what is happening has to exactly coincide with the image we have of ourselves. Simply said, our outer reality has to match our inner reality.

A good self-image will produce good decisions because it is universal law. It has to reflect who we believe ourselves to be and what we are worth. The only way to handle a perceived problem is with the knowledge that problems are all made up. Problems are created by us, by our negative self-image. For most, this is hard to accept, but we know that some of the problems we experience may be seen as blessings to others. This is because their self-image is one that empowers them based on their interpretation, solution, and course of action. There are no actual problems, just life events. Once we accept that, we can then center ourselves and clear ourselves each day so we can get rid of our negative self-image and tap into our positive self-image. This will create a reality that is empowering. A person with a positive self-image will have a life full of power, creativity, and love while a person with a negative self-image will have the opposite.

Once we create a positive self-image, our feelings about the situation will no longer be seen as a problem. Instead, we will be left with a choice to act or not act in a given situation. We won't worry about being judged because we will know our actions are right. If people find fault with our decision, we will know that it is because they have conjured up a "problem" based on their self-image.

Taking care of our self-image must be our number-one priority. It is the only way to happiness and the only way we can treat ourselves and others with respect and love.

Having a good self-image does not mean being egotistical. A person with a bloated ego is just as destructive as a person with low self-esteem.

A good self-image means we are balanced and centered. Serenity and humility are acquired because we will feel no better or worse than anyone else. We will be content to travel on our journey with a clear mind and a happy disposition. We will finally be able to truly enjoy our life because our positive self-image will closely mirror our personal truth, and this will reflect out into a beautiful reality worth living.

NOTES

"Your beliefs become your thoughts
Your thoughts become your words
Your words become your actions
Your actions become your destiny.

Mahatma Ghandi," he said. "There's more,
but I can't remember it all."
— Louise Penny, *A Fatal Grace*

AFFIRMATIONS

How can you go about effecting a real change in your life?

The only way to change what goes on outside you is to change what goes on inside you. Once you change your inner reality, your outer reality will automatically change.

There is no objective reality. Reality is based on how you are feeling inside. For example, if you feel good inside, then your outer reality will feel good, too. If you are feeling bad inside, then your outside reality will also feel bad.

Our life is like a motion picture that is acted out each moment and is constantly changing. This direction is the consequence or end result of all input, whether from others or originating from within, having to be filtered through our self-image *before* it becomes reality. Self-image is like tinted glasses. The more tinted the glasses, the more negative the reality will be. Our reality is always after the fact, determined by that filter of self-image.

One way to cause positive changes in our lives is through the affirmation process, which, when done properly, will create a more positive self image and set the stage for achieving desired results and a happier life.

Affirmations are positive statements that describe a desired situation or goal. They are repeated many times in order to affect the subconscious mind and trigger a positive action that will result in your being more content.

To be effective, affirmations must be repeated with great conviction and desire.

The beliefs we have are the truth. It doesn't matter to the subconscious mind if our beliefs are in fact true or not. You don't even have to believe the new positive message because your subconscious mind can't distinguish between what your conscious mind believes and what you are telling it to believe.

If we imagine a desired outcome with all our heart and soul and repeat it often enough, our subconscious will accept it as true and will have no choice but to create it.

Of course, this is also the case for negative thoughts. If you constantly think in terms of "I don't really deserve to be rich," "My friends will hate me if I become rich and they don't," "I am too stupid to talk in front of people," etc., your subconscious will accept that as your truth, and you will make decisions that ensure a negative outcome.

The subconscious mind can be trained to work for or against us. It is always there whether we are thinking about it or not. We need to stay alert of what we are feeding our mind. We need to keep our mind in tip-top shape through positive affirmations.

Always start an affirmation with "I will," or "I am," or another self-loving acknowledgment. Never start with "I can" or "I want" because those words imply a struggle and the possibility of a negative outcome. Always make positive affirmations that can have only one result with no room for failure. Examples would be "I will find a soul mate," "I will be rich," "I love myself unconditionally," and "I deserve to be happy." Visualize your affirmation as having already happened and being part of your life. The very best affirmations are ones that promote self-love and self-worth since those are the ones that affect all others.

If you want to lose weight, visualize yourself as fit and healthy. If you want to be rich, visualize yourself as surrounded by wealth. These images will be accepted as true by the subconscious mind. A vision board is also a good way to impress the subconscious mind. The more you believe in an affirmation, the more likely it is to happen. If you do not declare it, it will likely never happen, so why not start to make declarations today? For affirmations to be powerful you need to write them as specifically as possible and include a specific date. "I will have a girlfriend (be as specific as possible about what type of girl), and I will have her by January 1, 2012."

If you read these declarations daily, they will become part of your inner reality. Before you know it, they will manifest in your outer reality. Your outer reality, meaning your life, is a perfect reflection of your inner reality and the way you feel about yourself.

Once you practice affirmations on a daily basis, you will eventually find yourself, without conscious thought, to be doing the very things that will enable you to reach your goals. This cannot be any other way. The new, positive image of yourself will automatically be fulfilled.

NOTES

"You have power over your mind - not outside events. Realize this, and you will find strength."

— Marcus Aurelius, *Meditations*

Clearing
and Journalizing

Clearing is a concept used to protect yourself from the effects of stress on your thought process. Journalizing is one of the tools used to clear your mind. Stress produces a busy mind that stands in the way of clearly visualizing we want out of life. It is extremely difficult to think clearly when your mind is cluttered. Stress also creates an imbalance, which makes us vulnerable to addictions.

A stressed mind produces an unhealthy physical and mental state that can lead to disease and depression. Also, stress drives us into basing our decisions on random thoughts, which are fear-driven and usually not good for us. Eliminating scattered thoughts releases many of the fears that stand in the way of making clear decisions.

Journalizing will give those fragmented thoughts a path to be released and leave your mind free to solve problems in a rational, creative way. Journalizing is not a writing exercise but rather a mind clearing exercise.

Do not worry about style or content. Do not worry about spelling or penmanship. Start by writing anything that comes to mind, no matter how scattered, silly, or disconnected your thoughts may be at that moment. Just write whatever comes to mind as fast as the thoughts come with as little thought or analysis as possible.

Just as the body needs a daily clearing, so does the mind. Daily clearing will rid the mind of the frustration and busyness that block the clear, creative energy needed to live efficiently and be present in the moment. If journalizing is made a daily practice, it will soon become a trusted tool that will enable you to start each day with a clear and focused mind.

The best times of day to journalize are immediately after waking in the morning, at night before sleep, or whenever something is bothering you.

With the release of all that clutter in your head, the mind becomes clear. Clearing through journalizing will also make your life much more productive because you will be letting go of the thoughts and feelings that are in your way and hold you back. As you journalize, your life will become clear, happy, light, and full of joy and happiness. These moments of happiness will become more frequent as your journalizing becomes a daily habit.

NOTES

"Not all of us can do great things. But we can do small things with great love."
— Mother Teresa

"~Be the change you want to see in the world~"
— Mahatma Ghandi

Faith without Works Is Dead

I will not try to convince you of which God to believe in, but I will tell you that having faith has helped me so many times when I felt like just giving up. Over my years of coaching, I have seen people with no faith struggling as much as people who had faith but just wanted to sit back and have God do all the work.

I believe in God, but I do believe that we must do the legwork. As has been said many times, faith without works is dead. I believe that God loves us unconditionally. Our humanity gets in the way, and then we start to doubt the love that God has for us and our ability to love ourselves and others. It is our humanity that stops us from getting the life we love, not God. Responsibility, commitment, integrity, honor, and respect for ourselves and others are the foundation of creating that extraordinary life and a life we love.

The greatest level of joy for a father who loves his children is seeing them happy and living lives they love. So why not take that on and make your creator happy?

Start right now by making a commitment to yourself and to God that you will never give up until you create a life you love. I assure you that just by your making that commitment, your life will start to change.

NOTES

"This is your life and its ending one moment at a time."
— Chuck Palahniuk, *Fight Club*

MASTERING THE ILLUSION OF TIME

One of the biggest misconceptions we have is that the events in our lives have inevitable causes. This is because time flows in a seemingly continuous, step-by-step onward movement. To be trapped in this illusion is to feel helpless in changing the course of our lives.

In fact, time itself is an illusion necessary to experience this reality. Understanding this can be a great tool to alter our reality and destiny.

Time is nothing more than single frames of created reality that gives us the illusion of motion, just like a movie camera. Our minds take these single frames and process them at a speed that gives them what we call reality in the moment.

Our belief that the present creative moment must follow the previous one and continue is an illusion. There is no actual past since there is no actual flowing of time. Our minds remember past moments and ponder future moments all at the same point of consciousness. This is the illusion of the present moment.

Our reality is made up of three ideas of time all at once. Two of them, the past and future, are not actually happening at all but are made up by the only one that is really happening, the present moment. That is why we have ultimate control of our destiny. We cause everything that happens to us in our lives, because it can be no other way. Everything that occurs is a result of the choices we make in the present moment throughout our lives.

If, through habitual negative thinking, we lose sight of the power of the creative present moment, then we trap ourselves into believing we are victims of outside forces and cannot change the course of our lives. In fact, we are victims of the illusion we created of the past or the future. We then become feathers, blown in whatever direction the wind takes us.

To seize the present moment and direct the course of our own lives is to be an arrow, sprung from the bow of our creative force on an unwavering mission toward whatever goal we seek. So seize the present moment now and be the master of your life.

NOTES

"Twenty years from now you will be more disappointed by the things that you didn't do than by the ones you did do. So throw off the bowlines. Sail away from the safe harbor. Catch the trade winds in your sails. Explore. Dream. Discover."
— H. Jackson Brown Jr.

"Each night, when I go to sleep, I die. And the next morning, when I wake up, I am reborn."
— Mahatma Gandhi

THE END IS
THE BEGINNING

When I started my journey, I thought I would arrive someplace, be happy, and then live happily ever after. I soon realized that I was wrong. Spiritual practices teach us that happiness is a journey, not a destination, and that we will never arrive. It is in the creation of each moment that life happens.

There is only this moment—not yesterday, not tomorrow, but *now*.

Happiness is not a destination to get to but an awareness that we are already there.

We strive so much to get someplace. We want the car, the money, the degree, and the significant other only to get them and be happy for a moment. We then go back into wanting more and more, and we spend our lives living that way. Why not be happy *now*?

Making commitments, setting goals, and having dreams are very important parts of our happiness.

Accomplishing these tasks or reaching these destinations does not constitute happiness. Rather, the journey of going toward these goals, dreams, and commitments is what will make us happy. The practice of understanding that each moment is already extraordinary is where happiness is realized.

One of the greatest wisdoms in creating an extraordinary life and a life that I love is understanding that I already have an extraordinary life.

CONTACT INFORMATION

Andrea Colandrea Life Coaching Company
For personal coaching or business coaching, call 516-647-7998.
E-mail: Colandreaandrea1@yahoo.com

Andrea is available to speak at your place of

- business;
- group;
- fundraiser;
- organization;
- school;
- college campus;
- community center;
- or any other function.

For more information, call Andrea Colandrea at 516-647-7998.

NOTES

Andrea Colandrea & Bob Lembo

Andrea Colandrea & Bob Lembo

About the Authors

Andrea Colandrea was born in Italy and moved to New York when he was ten years old. He has been an entrepreneur for the past twenty-three years. His journey to creating an extraordinary life began when he got divorced in February 2001. His journey to understand why he was unhappy in his life is what inspired him to write this book. This book is about how he went from a life he hated to a life he loves and calls extraordinary. Andrea Colandrea continues to share his strategies in creating an extraordinary life through being a life coach and motivational speaker.

Bob Lembo was born in the Bronx in 1943. He has been a lifelong social activist and health advocate. In recent years he has focused his energy on helping those who have allowed their loving self-image to be covered with self-doubt, leading to a depressive reality.

"Success is getting what you want. Happiness is wanting what you get."—Dale Carnegie

Traci Chiarello (Project Manager) graduated from the University of North Carolina at Charlotte and now works full-time in Real Estate. She grew up in Massapequa, NY. Her main focus these days is to create an extraordinary life with her soon to be husband.

"Success or Failure in business is caused more by mental attitude even than by mental capacities."—Walter Scott.